GO FACTS FOOD

From Farms to You

A & C BLACK • LONDON

From Farms to You

contents

© Blake Publishing 2003
Additional material © A & C Black Publishers Ltd 2005

First published 2003 in Australia by Blake Education Pty Ltd

This edition published 2005 in the United Kingdom by
A & C Black Publishers Ltd, 37 Soho Square, London W1D 3QZ
www.acblack.com

ISBN-10: 0-7136-7290-0
ISBN-13: 978-0-7136-7290-9

A CIP record for this book is available from the British Library.

Written by Paul McEvoy
Design and layout by The Modern Art Production Group
Photos by John Foxx, Photodisc, Brand X, Corbis, Digital Stock,
Eyewire and Artville.

UK series consultant: Julie Garnett

Printed in China by WKT Company Ltd.

A & C Black uses paper produced with elemental chlorine-free pulp,
harvested from managed sustainable forests.

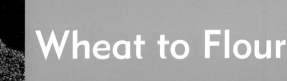

Processed Food

Some foods go through many changes before they get to your table.

Some of the food we buy is fresh, such as fruit, vegetables, meat, eggs and fish. Other foods are cooked or changed in some way. These are known as **processed** foods.

Most food is processed in factories. Some processes, like drying, freezing and canning, **preserve** food. Other processes cook and combine foods. The food is then **packaged** in cans, jars, boxes, bottles or frozen packs. Then it is sent to shops and supermarkets.

Workers process corn in a factory.

Pears can be cooked with sugar and water and then bottled.

Supermarkets sell many processed foods.

5

Cows to Milk

How does cows' milk become ready to drink?

1. **Dairy** cows need plenty of grass and fresh water to make milk.

2. Cows are milked in sheds using milking machines.

3. Milk tankers take the milk to a factory. The milk is heated to kill any harmful **bacteria**.

4. The milk is put into bottles or cartons and kept refrigerated. Then it is taken to shops and supermarkets.

Berries to Jam

Berries can be eaten fresh. They can also be cooked with sugar to make jam.

1 Berries grow on small bushes or plants in fields and hothouses.

2 Some farmers use machines to harvest the ripe berries. Others are picked by hand.

3 The berries are washed, trimmed and cut up or mashed. Then the berries are cooked with sugar until the mixture is thick.

4 Next the hot jam is poured into jars and **sealed** to keep it fresh.

Bees to Honey

Bees make honey. People only need to collect and bottle it.

1. Beekeepers build **hives** for their bees.

2. Honey bees collect **nectar** from flowers. They carry it back to the hive.

3. Inside the hive are wax honeycombs. Worker bees process the nectar. As the nectar dries, it becomes honey.

4. To collect the honey, beekeepers wear protective clothing and face nets to avoid stings. The honey is **strained** and put into jars or bottles.

Wheat to Flour

How are grains of wheat made into flour?

1. Farmers grow wheat crops in large fields.

2. **Combine harvesters** cut the wheat plants and separate the grains.

3. Trucks or trains take the wheat to the **mill** where it is ground into flour.

4. The flour is packaged and sent to bakeries or supermarkets.

Flour to Pasta

Pasta and noodles can be made from flour at home or in factories.

1 Flour is mixed with water, and sometimes eggs and other **ingredients**, into a firm dough.

2 The dough is rolled out.

3 It is forced through holes in a machine to make spaghetti or other shapes. The pasta dries and hardens.

4 Before you eat it, pasta is cooked in boiling water to make it soft.

Tomatoes to Sauce

Some tomatoes are cooked to make tomato sauce for pasta.

1 Tomatoes grow on tall plants. They are often picked when they are green. Tomatoes will turn red after being picked.

2 Tomato sauce can be made at home. The tomatoes are skinned, then chopped or **puréed**.

3 Next, the chopped tomatoes are cooked with other ingredients such as water, salt, spices, meat or vegetables.

4 The sauce can be served with pasta or in other dishes.

1

2

3

4

From Farms to You

Glossary

bacteria	germs that can cause disease
combine harvester	a machine that cuts and sorts grain
dairy	related to producing milk or milk products
hive	a container to house honey bees
ingredient	item added to a mixture
mill	a building where grain is crushed
nectar	a sweet food from plants
package	put into a container or wrap to sell
preserve	prepare food for use in the future
processed	changed by cooking or other actions
purée	grind or crush into a paste
seal	close tightly so air cannot get in
strain	pour through fine holes to get rid of lumps

Index

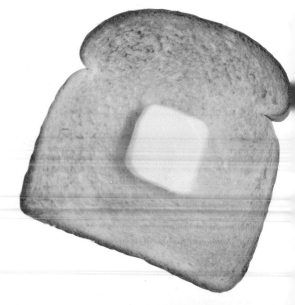